M000164187

BE MORE

BER

COW

BE MORE BER COW

EMBRACE YOUR INNER JOHN
AND GET YOUR LIFE IN ORR-DERRRRR!

First published in Great Britain in 2019 by Atlantic Books,
an imprint of Atlantic Books Ltd.

10 9 8 7 6 5 4 3 2 1

A CIP catalogue record for this book is available from the
British Library. Every effort has been made to trace or contact
all copyright holders. The publishers will be pleased to make
good any omissions or rectify any mistakes brought to their
attention at the earliest opportunity.

Hardback ISBN 978 1 83895 026 2

Designed by Yes/No Publishing

Printed in Malta by Gutenberg Press Ltd.
Atlantic Books
An Imprint of Atlantic Books Ltd
Ormond House
26–27 Boswell Street
London
WC1N 3JZ

www.atlantic-books.co.uk

This book belongs to

....

NAMASTE
WELCOME
WILLKOMMEN
BIENVENU

Gauge where you are at the beginning of your quest to Be More Bercow, and mark the following statements on a scale of 1 to 10 (with 1 being you strongly disagree with the statement and 10 being you strongly agree with the statement).

I am able to make myself heard at work meetings and social gatherings.

Disagree   Agree

1   2   3   4   5   6   7   8   9   10

Colleagues consider me a confident and able executor of tasks and duties.

Disagree   Agree

1   2   3   4   5   6   7   8   9   10

I am comfortable in the company of strangers.

Disagree   Agree

1   2   3   4   5   6   7   8   9   10

I am happy to spend my days shouting 'Orr-derr!' at unruly individuals.

Disagree   Agree

1   2   3   4   5   6   7   8   9   10

Danny Dyer would make a great successor to John Bercow as Mr Speaker.

Disagree   Agree

1   2   3   4   5   6   7 · 8   9   10

'Stick to your abacus, man.'

John Bercow,
February 2018

To understand Bercow is to become Bercow

THE
PARABLES
OF JOHN

THE TAXI DRIVER'S SON

Born in north London in 1963 to Brenda and taxi-driving Charles, John Simon Bercow is the grandson of Romanian Jewish immigrants. John attended a comprehensive school in North Finchley, and then went on to earn a first-class honours degree in government from the University of Essex. John's spare time at university would have been much more likely to involve Arsenal football club, as opposed to the exclusive Bullingdon Club of Oxford that future Conservative Party leaders David Cameron and Boris Johnson attended in their university days.

Much has been written about the supposed 'old school tie' bias within the Tory party, and with another Old Etonian leading the party again, there is plenty of food for thought. Perhaps having someone from a 'bog-standard comprehensive' as Speaker is helping even things up a little.

'For far too long the House of Commons has been run as little more than a private club by and for gentleman amateurs.'

John Bercow,
from a letter to the *Independent,* May 2009

'This "kiss a ginger" activity is probably perfectly lawful, but I have got no plans to partake of it myself. It strikes me as a very rum business altogether.'

John Bercow,
January 2017

International Kiss a Ginger Day has been running on the 12th of January since 2009, and if like John it strikes you as a 'very rum business' and you do not 'wish to partake', then why not celebrate by getting your lips around this ginger cocktail, which is also very rum.

THE KISS A GINGER COCKTAIL

50 ml of white rum
100 ml of ginger beer
A few leaves of mint
The juice of half a lime

Fill a glass with ice, then add the rum, lime and mint.
Pour over the ginger beer and kiss that ginger!

Test your
ability to…

ASSERT YOURSELF

If the Speaker stands, then MPs are required to sit.
Try using this assertiveness technique in your everyday life.

Take a bus ride. Stand up from your seat
and make somebody else sit in it.

Explore this strategy in other seated environments,
such as the theatre or a restaurant.

Try standing up in the middle of the forest to
see if your assertiveness makes wildlife sit.

How did it make you feel? How did it make them feel?

Congratulations –
you're one step closer to becoming more Bercow.

RISE ABOVE ADVERSITY

Back in 1996, long before John Bercow was elected Speaker of the House, this ambitious young Tory upstart found an ingenious solution to an everyday problem – how to be in two places at the same time. Needing to attend two separate selection meetings for two safe Conservative parliamentary seats almost simultaneously, he spent £1,000 on chartering a helicopter to make the 80-mile journey in minutes rather than the hours that the same journey would have taken him by car.

Perhaps impressed by his drive and determination, or by his money, Bercow was confirmed as the candidate for the Buckingham constituency, and was duly elected as an MP in the general election of 1997.

WHAT CAN WE LEARN FROM THIS STORY?

When the going gets tough,
the tough get going?

Necessity is the mother of invention?

It is easier for a camel to
go through the eye of a needle
than for a rich man to get into heaven?

OR

If you throw money at things,
sometimes you get what you want?

'Others can proceed as they wish, but I have never been pushed around and I am not going to start now.'

John Bercow,
March 2019

In the tempestuous waters of our modern lives, it is important to remain firm as the waves crash against you. The next time events in your professional or public life conspire against you, imagine yourself as a curmudgeonly Bercow barnacle, clinging on to a stable rock as the tsunami rampages around you.

If you can cling on to the rock for almost a decade then like Mr Speaker you might find yourself with a reward such as a bottle of wine or a peerage. Or not, as the case may be!

DARE TO SOAR!

John Bercow is assertive, brave and unapologetic.

What other characteristics does John Bercow have that you could emulate to allow yourself the freedom to fly and achieve your dreams? Write them in the clouds opposite and then prioritize them.

And if it makes it any easier, then do as
John did and hire a helicopter to help you!

THE LGBTQ+ MANDALA

John Bercow is proud to support equal rights for the LGBTQ+ community, and as such has incorporated the pink triangle as a positive symbol of solidarity into his personal coat of arms.

When you need a bit more calm and order in your life, be more Bercow and focus your attentions on this mandala inspired by the pink triangle symbol and the rainbow flag of the LGBTQ+ community.

'We could have a debate on the definition of happiness. I will offer a starter for ten: victories for Arsenal football club and Roger Federer.'

John Bercow,
March 2019

For Mr Speaker, the definition of happiness seems
quite clear, but what defines happiness for you?

In the space below list ten things that
bring you joy and next time you are feeling
down rewrite that list in your mind.

·   ·

·   ·

·   ·

· · · · · · · · · · · · · · · · · · ·   ·

· · · · · · · · · · · · · · · · · ·   ·

RELAX

**Adopt a dignified posture
and then study this picture of John Bercow.**

Notice three things about the photo.

.... / .... / ....

Notice three things about how you feel.

.... / .... / ....

Notice three things about your breathing.

.... / .... / ....

**Live in this moment
and immerse yourself in Bercow.**

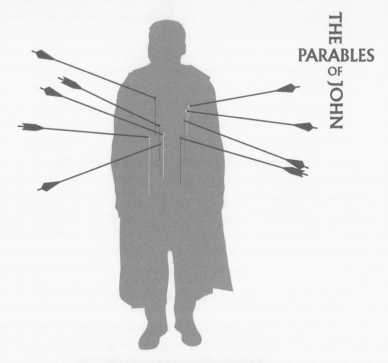

MARTYR TO THE CAUSE

Once upon a Bercow, when the notion of J.B.'s election to the role of Mr Speaker was just a twinkle in the eye of his parliamentary colleagues, he made an honourable and virtuous sacrifice for his ideals. In November 2002, the then Leader of the Opposition, Iain Duncan Smith, imposed a three-line whip on his Tory members to oppose the Labour government's Adoption and Children Act. This proposed allowing unmarried couples, both heterosexual and same-sex, to adopt children, which until then hadn't been legal. Refusing to toe the party line, Bercow voted with the Labour government and then promptly resigned from the front bench, incurring the wrath of his party leader, but securing his reputation as a man of principle and a maverick.

WHAT CAN WE LEARN FROM THIS STORY?

You must stand up for what you believe in,
no matter what the personal cost?

What goes around comes around and
good things come to those who wait?

There is no pot of gold at the end of the rainbow?

OR

Iain Duncan Smith maybe wasn't the
best Leader of the Opposition ever?

'The honourable member for Rhondda is chuntering from a sedentary position, "Meet with you." It seems to be his preferred mantra of the day.'

John Bercow,
October 2018

MANTRA OF THE DAY

There is 'chuntering from a sedentary position', and then there is performing a considered life-enriching mantra. Be more Bercow and set out a few preferred mantras that you can incorporate into your day.

WITH ORDER COMES CONTENTMENT

....

....

....

'HAVING A BAD DAY?' 'EVERYTHING GOT ON TOP OF YOU?' 'LOST YOURSELF?'

Imagine John Bercow as a martial arts guru; enter the Bercow Mojo Dojo, heed the Bercow quotes and re-channel your inner energy.

Calm yourself.

Take up yoga.

Think Zen, restraint, patience.

Get a grip, man.

Let it go.

Now you will be ready to do battle with anything your
house, or any House for that matter, throws at you.

B**CKS TO BREXIT**
IT'S NOT A DONE DEAL

When the Conservative MP Adam Holloway addressed Mr Speaker during Prime Minister's Questions referring to a sticker 'in your car' with 'derogatory comments about Brexit', John Bercow was naturally affronted. The accusation stemmed from a widely distributed photo of a car, allegedly owned by him, that had a sticker affixed to the rear-view mirror with the campaign slogan 'B****cks to Brexit, it's not a done deal' emblazoned on it.

Interrupting the MP in mid-flow, Mr Speaker explained the error of Mr Holloway's ways. 'That sticker on the subject of Brexit happens to be affixed to, or in the windscreen of, my wife's car. Yes, it is. I am sure the honourable gentleman would not suggest for one moment that a wife is somehow the property or chattel of her husband. She is entitled to her views. That sticker is not mine, and that is the end of it.'

WHAT CAN WE LEARN FROM THIS STORY?

To assume is to make an ass out of 'u' and 'me'?

Don't believe everything you read in the media?

Maybe Donald Trump is right about 'fake news'?

OR

You should probably get your facts straight
before you stand on the national stage and try
to take down one of the nation's premier orators?

'I'm just being me. It's not a contrivance. It's not a put-on show. It's the way I am.'

John Bercow,
Der Spiegel, April 2019

ALWAYS REMAIN TRUE TO YOURSELF*

*EVEN IF YOU ARE INCREDIBLY LOUD AND RUB CERTAIN PEOPLE UP THE WRONG WAY!

ORDER

In the lobby to the left list all the things
in your life you are **NOT** content with.

··································

··································

··································

··································

··································

Once you have filled the lobbies with your thoughts ...

YOUR AFFAIRS

In the lobby to the right list all the things
in your life you are content with.

AYES

....

....

....

....

....

'UNLOCK!' the results and declare a winner.

'ORR-DUHH.'

THE
FOUR PILLARS
OF ORDER

No. 2
The Pointed Order

**Normally directed towards a particularly
rowdy Member of Parliament.**

As in,

'ORR-DUHH. You are an incorrigible delinquent.'

Or,

**'ORR-DUHH. You may be a cheeky chappie,
but you are also an exceptionally noisy one.'**

'I am always inclined to say, "Don't panic." I am not in the business of panicking myself.'

John Bercow,
March 2019

DON'T PANIC

Lance Corporal Jones of the BBC sitcom *Dad's Army* was famous for his call 'Don't panic, Mr Mainwaring' and John Bercow might have declared 'Don't panic, Mrs May', but is there anyone you know who would benefit from this kind of advice in these trying times?

Write their name in the space below.

DON'T PANIC, ...

John Bercow needs a loud voice to make himself heard in the House. But how can he be so confident?

Learn to free yourself from your inhibitions by behaving like a bovine beast –

A BER-COW

In a quiet room get on your hands and knees and allow yourself to breathe deeply.

When you are ready release a loud and confident

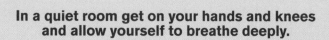

BER-COW MOO!

MOo

Feel how the deep rumbling sound reverberates around the room.

Now louder...

MOoOOoOO

Feel how your breath supports your voice.

And finally...

MOoOOoO-OOoOOoOO

Feel your confidence grow with the volume.

Now take what you have learnt into *your* house and fill it with bravado.

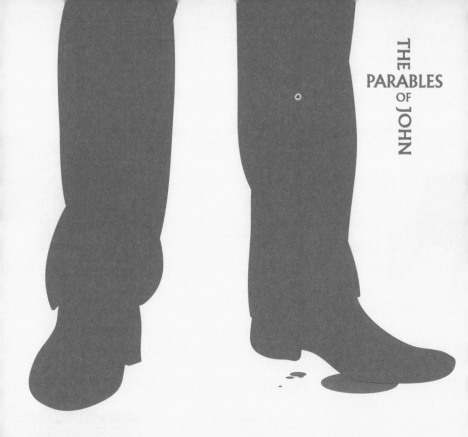

BE THE BIGGER PERSON

As reported in an April 2013 article in the *New York Times*, back in the summer of 2010 the then Hon. Simon Burns MP had called Mr Speaker a 'stupid, sanctimonious little dwarf' on the House of Commons floor. Apart from being very rude, interest groups representing people with dwarfism complained and Mr Burns promptly apologized 'to any group of people' he might have upset. But no such apology was forthcoming to the object of his derision, John Bercow.

Discussing the incident in the same *New York Times* article, John Bercow took the higher ground and displayed a textbook example of 'being the bigger person', declaring…

'I don't want to crawl over the entrails of past disputes.'

John Bercow,
New York Times, April 2013

'I think I can safely say that I have never lost a wink of sleep over any work-related matter.'

John Bercow,
March 2019

MINDFUL SLUMBER

Recent studies have shown how important sleep can be in maintaining a healthy lifestyle, but if, unlike Mr Speaker, you are not getting your full eight hours a night, what can you do about it? On the page below take a look at the common worries that might keep you up at night, and in the space provided assign a positive phrase that you can use to rationalize each worry.

At work you have an important presentation to make in front of all of your colleagues.

· ·

At home you have noticed some cracks on the internal walls that seem to be getting worse.

· ·

At work you have unearthed a centuries-old precedent to block the reading of a massively important bill about which you have received substantial criticism.

· ·

JOHN BERCOW IS RENOWNED FOR HIS COLLECTION OF COLOURFUL TIES

As you may know, colours can represent our moods and emotions. On the opposite page draw a line to match the tie colours to the event you might be facing.

Choose your tie wisely to remain right and honourable.

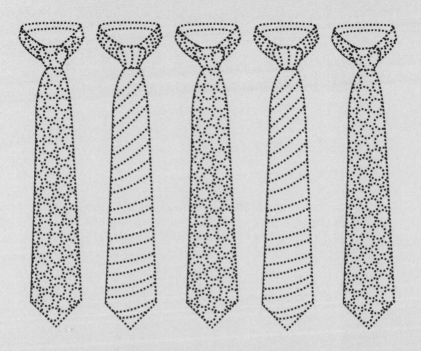

RED · · · · · · · · · · Cold and ruthless as you
negotiate a deal

BLUE · Fiery and dominant in an
important interview

YELLOW Comforting and calming as
you deliver some bad news

PINK Impartial as you chair a rowdy
debate on amendments to a
controversial Brexit plan

MULTI COLOURED Bright and sunny as you
relax with a loved one

If

by Rudyard Kipling

If you can keep your head when all about you
Are losing theirs and blaming it on you,
If you can trust yourself when all men doubt you,
But make allowance for their doubting too;
If you can wait and not be tired by waiting,
Or being lied about, don't deal in lies,
Or being hated, don't give way to hating,
And yet don't look too good, nor talk too wise:

If you can dream – and not make dreams your master;
If you can think – and not make thoughts your aim;
If you can meet with Triumph and Disaster
And treat those two impostors just the same;
If you can bear to hear the truth you've spoken
Twisted by knaves to make a trap for fools,
Or watch the things you gave your life to, broken,
And stoop and build 'em up with worn-out tools:

If you can make one heap of all your winnings
And risk it on one turn of pitch-and-toss,
And lose, and start again at your beginnings
And never breathe a word about your loss;
If you can force your heart and nerve and sinew
To serve your turn long after they are gone,
And so hold on when there is nothing in you
Except the Will which says to them: 'Hold on!'

If you can talk with crowds and keep your virtue,
Or walk with Kings – nor lose the common touch,
If neither foes nor loving friends can hurt you,
If all men count with you, but none too much;
If you can fill the unforgiving minute
With sixty seconds' worth of distance run,
Yours is the Earth and everything that's in it,
And – which is more – you'll be a Man, my son!

'Calm yourself, man – the lion must get back in its den.'

John Bercow,
January 2014

If, in your work life or at home, you find yourself amongst lions, calmly and authoritatively

'ORR-DERR'

them back into their den.

RELAX

**Adopt a dignified posture
and then study this picture of Boris Johnson.**

Notice three things about the photo.

.... / .... / ....

Notice three things about how you feel.

.... / .... / ....

Notice three things about your breathing.

.... / .... / ....

**Live in this moment
and immerse yourself in Johnson.**

BERCOW THE YOUNGISH

When the Rt. Hon. Member for Buckingham made his bid for
election as the new Speaker of the House back in 2009, he
relayed an approach he had made to an unidentified colleague
for support. He asked if the colleague would back him,
and he was met with the following reply:

'Certainly not, Bercow. You are not just too young; you are far too
young... the Speaker ought to be virtually senile. If you were
elected, it would be disastrous for you, disastrous for the
House, and disastrous for the country.'

As it turned out, Bercow was elected at the age of 46,
the youngest Speaker for over a century.

'Even youngish men can acquire wisdom as time goes by.'

John Bercow,
June 2009

'**I don't set out to cause controversy. I set out to do the right thing.'**

John Bercow,
Der Spiegel, April 2019

Consider the life lessons of other people that
have caused controversy by trying to do
what they thought was the right thing.

Neville Chamberlain

Theresa May

Jeremy Corbyn

David Cameron

David Icke

What can we learn from this?

Test your
ability to...

BE
HEARD

John Bercow uses the strength of his
voice to command a room and let it
be known that parliamentary process
will be adhered to. Learn to engage
your diaphragm and therefore
control the volume of your voice.

Repeat these phrases fifty times over,
ten times a day for three weeks:

'DEBATING NEEDS ORD-AHHH'

'ORDER IS NOT A FACT, IT'S A PROCESS'

'TAKE SOME MEDICAMENT'

**Concentrate on enunciation and
increasing the volume as you go.**

**Now find a particularly noisy environment where
there are many opposing opinions being expressed
at once, a Labour Party conference perhaps.
Place a friend or colleague on the opposite side
of the crowd and try to be heard above the din.**

Were you successful?

Yes   No

**If yes then congratulations,
you're one step closer to becoming more Bercow.**

THE ARSENAL MANDALA

Mr Speaker is a lifelong supporter of north London football team Arsenal, regularly shoehorning adulatory comments about their performance into general Commons banter.

When you need a bit more calm and order in your life, be more Bercow and focus your attentions on this mandala inspired by the team's crest.

'Reform, not revolution.'

John Bercow,
Washington Post, May 2019

The UK Parliament has a grand tradition of reform, not revolution. The First Reform Act of 1832 paved the way for a more equal distribution of MPs, and went some way in abolishing 'rotten boroughs'. But what reforms could you make in your life that might help you be more Bercow?

Make a list of everyday personal parliamentary 'Acts' that will help you reform, not revolutionize.

We've added a few examples below to help you on your way.

THE 'MOBILE DEVICES DOWN AFTER 9PM' ACT
....

THE 'IT'S NOT OK TO FINISH
THE BOTTLE NOW IT'S OPEN' ACT
....

....

....

....

....

....

IMAGINE YOURSELF MAROONED ON AN ISLAND

How long were you able to last without stating an opinion?

· ·

How annoying was it that no one
was there to listen to your opinion?

· ·

How did you go about redecorating
the island to your personal taste?

· ·

Now close your eyes and imagine the blissful calm and order on the island. Maybe you have built a House of Commons sandcastle? Perhaps you are chairing a debate between the wild boars on the right and the crabs on the left.

JOHN BERCOW, SUPERSTAR

It has been said that not much good has come out of Brexit so far, no matter which side of the fence you sit. But from an international standpoint, the focus of all the attention has not been on Theresa May, Jeremy Corbyn or Boris Johnson. No, the spotlight has fallen on the holder of what has traditionally been a fairly anonymous bit-part role, Speaker of the House of Commons.

Fascinated by the quaint traditions, curious language and the hammed-up drama, John Bercow has become a household name in many countries around the world. He is described in the Dutch newspaper *De Volkskrant* as 'Louder, boisterous and, yes, more animal than ever' and the journalist goes on to suggest 'the only order in British politics comes from John Bercow's mouth in these turbulent days'. In Belgium's *Le Soir* he is often described as 'unbearable, but irreplaceable', and in the *Washington Post* as 'the most theatrical, sharp-tongued and proactive speaker in modern time'. Yes, John Bercow is fast on his way to becoming an international superstar.

WHAT CAN WE LEARN FROM THIS STORY?

Bad news travels fast?

Every cloud has a silver lining?

OR

If his legacy doesn't extend to a peerage, then a fully booked schedule on the international public speaking circuit might suffice?

'The honourable gentleman has got to learn the art of patience, and if he is patient, if he deploys Zen, he will find it is ultimately to everyone's advantage.'

John Bercow,
January 2019

CONSIDER...

If all members of the House of Commons had been more Bercow and deployed Zen, would the Brexit debates have gone the way they did?

ACTION...

To inject some order into a family get-together or a business meeting, suggest everyone adopts the lotus position and considers their own breathing. Why not lead a meditation and see if you can inject some order into what follows?

FENG SHUI IN THE HOUSE

Put simply, feng shui is the art of arranging objects in your environment in a way that might affect your success, health and happiness.

Imagine you are John Bercow, feng shui master, famous for bringing order and prosperity to the House of Commons.

Consider the secrets of your success.

Was it the positioning instructions of the mace that you gave to the Serjeant at Arms?

Was it the scheduling of a long debate to coincide with the tidal surge in the Thames?

Was it the clever redistribution and fluffing of the parliamentary cushions shortly before PMQs?

**Be more Bercow and imagine how you could apply feng shui
to increase the order and prosperity in your house.**

**Think of three things to rearrange
and record your results here.**

....

....

....

'ORRR-DAAA-HHHH.'

THE
FOUR PILLARS
OF ORDER

No. 3
The Authoritarian Order

Mr Speaker's trademark bellow, used to call
the House to attention, and his most-often
used of all four pillars of order.

As in,

'ORRR-DAAAHHHH. The House must calm itself.'

Or,

'ORRR-DAAAHHHH. There is simply
too much noise in the chamber on both sides.'

'Well, I am glad she is an Arsenal supporter, but she still should not chunter. As she represents West Ham, she might find it therapeutic to blow some bubbles.'

John Bercow,
February 2017

THERAPY BUBBLES

In the bubbles below write a word or two to describe some things that are bothering you. Then, when you are ready, take an imaginary sharp object and for each one 'put a pin in it'. Pop those worrisome bubbles!

FINDING YOUR VOICE

Consider the power of John Bercow's
voice, its timbre and resonance.

How does this help him convey his feeling and thoughts?

• •

Compare your voice to his.

What areas can you work on to emulate how he speaks?

• •

Do you need more clarity, more depth, more volume?

• •

Work on these aspects until you are satisfied
that you have achieved Bercow's trademark growl.

Repeating the phrase

'YOU WILL OBEY THE COURTESIES OF THE HOUSE',

try out these different styles of speaking.

**See how comfortable they feel
then score yourself out of ten.**

☐ **Shakespearean actor**

☐ **Builder**

☐ **Loyd Grossman**

☐ **Scurvy knave**

☐ **Radio disc jockey**

☐ **Stable lad**

SHOULD I STAY OR SHOULD I GO?

'Should I leave or remain?' is a curiously recurring question of Mr Speaker's political career.

In 2002, disagreeing with the Tory party's three-line whip to oppose a new bill enabling unmarried and same-sex couples to adopt children, he resigned from the front bench.

Leave   **Remain** ☐

In 2007, despite very strong rumours to the contrary, John Bercow decided not to defect to the Labour Party and remained a Conservative MP.

Leave ☐   **Remain**

In 2019, ignoring accusations of partiality in favour of Remain over his handling of Brexit, he has (at times a little uncomfortably) tried to remain sitting on the fence.

Leave   **Remain**

The last part of his fourth tenure as Mr Speaker has seen the constant questioning of when he should step down from his role. For the time being he remains, stating that it is 'not sensible to vacate the chair' while Brexit remains unresolved.

Leave ☐   **Remain**

WHAT CAN WE LEARN FROM THESE MOMENTS?

Sometimes it is harder to stay
than seek out new opportunities?

If I go there will be trouble?

If I stay it will be double?

OR

Sitting on the fence over Brexit is great when you
are an independent arbiter of the parliamentary process,
but maybe not if you are the Leader of the Opposition?

'I do not want
to be someone;
I want to do
something.'

John Bercow,
June 2009

DO SOMETHING

**Write a list of 'somethings' you want to do,
and tick them off once you have done them!**

SOMETHING

☐

....

☐

....

☐

....

☐

....

☐

....

☐

....

☐

....

☐

....

☐

....

☐

....

Be more Bercow and try to connect the following
opposite forces that exist in Mr Speaker's House.

YIN

YANG

Labour

Disorder

Noes

Unlock

Jeremy Corbyn

Remain

Leave

Conservative

Order

Ayes

Lock

Boris Johnson

Be more Bercow and list five pairs of opposite forces in your house. Consider how these may complement each other.

YIN

YANG

....

....

....

....

....

....

....

....

....

....

THE ESSEX MANDALA

Having graduated from and then subsequently been appointed as Chancellor of the University of Essex, John Bercow is proud to incorporate the elements of the flag of Essex into his own personal coat of arms.

When you need a bit more calm and order in your life, be more Bercow and focus your attentions on this mandala inspired by the flag of Essex and the proud crest of its university.

'You are over-excitable and you need to contain yourself – if it requires you to take some medicament then so be it.'

John Bercow,
April 2018

We all get over-excited sometimes: at a sporting event, on our birthdays, in the pub discussing Brexit with our friends. But when we need to calm down we don't always have a soothing tonic on hand. So why not make your own mindful medicament that you will always have with you to drink from when the need arises.

Ingredients

1   imaginary empty bottle with a cork

1   memory of a tranquil and peaceful moment (e.g. sipping a cocktail on a beach)

Method

1. Immerse yourself in the memory for 10 minutes

2. Distil this memory into an imaginary concentrated liquid

3. Uncork the imaginary bottle and decant the imaginary tonic inside

4. Re-cork the imaginary bottle and label for future reference

VOILA!

Your very own bottle of

MINDFUL MEDICAMENT.

RELAX

**Adopt a dignified posture
and then study this picture of Jeremy Corbyn.**

Notice three things about the photo.

.... / .... / ....

Notice three things about how you feel.

.... / .... / ....

Notice three things about your breathing.

.... / .... / ....

**Live in this moment
and immerse yourself in Corbyn.**

SOMETHING OF THE NIGHT ABOUT HIM

Not too long before John Bercow was elected as Speaker of the House, he was a rising star in the Conservative Party. But as his politics swung away from the right and towards the not so right, he began to slip from favour, and seemingly lose the appetite to ingratiate himself before the party kingmakers. So much so that by 2004, just after he had managed to claw his way back onto the front bench in the role of Shadow Secretary of State for International Development, he allegedly agreed with his Conservative colleague Ann Widdecombe that there was 'something of the night' about Michael Howard MP. There were two problems with this comment: the first being that Michael Howard was at that time the Leader of the Conservative Party, and the second being that John Bercow allegedly said it directly to Michael Howard.

John Bercow was fired immediately and his role of 'rising star' of the party was altered arguably to that of 'thorn in the side' of the party.

WHAT CAN WE LEARN FROM THIS STORY?

You can't fit a square peg in a round hole?

You reap what you sow?

Feel the fear and do it anyway,
and destiny will decide your path?

OR

Ann Widdecombe's talent for coining a catchy phrase is significantly better than her 'talent' on the dance floor?

'My approach is to try to facilitate, perhaps by enabling the fullest and fairest expression of views.'

John Bercow,
Der Spiegel, April 2019

EXPRESS YOURSELF

Sometimes the greatest gift you can bestow is to nurture the growth of expression.

Where in your everyday life can you facilitate a full and fair expression of views?

Challenge yourself in the following scenarios to see if you can be more Bercow:

☐ **Around the water cooler at work**

☐ **In the back of a taxi**

☐ **During a discussion about Brexit with your in-laws**

☐ **On the terraces during a match**

☐ **On the night bus**

☐ **In a library**

LET'S SPEAK BERCOWESE

John Bercow is renowned for his interesting turns of phrase. On the following page see if you can find more interesting, Bercow-inspired ways of delivering each sentence.

Here's one to get you started...

The cow jumped over the moon

THE OXEN HURDLED THE ORB OF NIGHT

A piece of cake

....

Barking up the wrong tree

....

You can lead a horse to water

....

Member of the House of Commons

....

By exploring the extremes of your vocabulary
you too can soon be talking fluent Bercowese.

'ORR-DERR. ORR-DERR. BUT, ORR-DERR.'

THE
FOUR PILLARS
OF ORDER

No. 4
The Desperate Order

**Most commonly used at the end of a long session,
when it seems that, to use a sporting metaphor,
Mr Speaker has lost the dressing room.**

As in,

**'Orr-derr. Orr-derr. But, orr-derr.
You're yelling across the chamber. Be quiet.'**

Or,

**'Orr-derr. Orr-derr. But, orr-derr.
I don't know what has happened.'**

'I absolutely promise you that I have never practised "put-downs". It's spontaneous. It's just what comes to me at the time.'

John Bercow,
Washington Post, May 2019

Mr Speaker is renowned for his quick-witted banter and spontaneous repartee. Let your confidence flourish and add a little sprinkling of verbal freestyling to your life. In the spaces below try out a few pithy responses to these potentially destabilizing everyday comments.

'You look like you've been dragged through a hedge backwards.'

. . . .

'You're alright, Jack – pull the ladder up!'

. . . .

'There's something of the night about you.'

. . . .

REMAIN!

LEAVE!

Test your
ability to...

SHOW
RESTRAINT

Although you, like John Bercow, may be opinionated,
it's important to hold your tongue when necessary.
Especially if you're chairing a national debate.

Deliberately locate yourself amongst people whose opinions you violently disagree with. If you are a Remainer then maybe have a pint with Nigel Farage. If a Leaver then perhaps share a taxi with Alastair Campbell.

How long were you able to last without stating an opinion?

• •

Were you able to remain calm in the heat of the moment?

• •

Were you able to control your emotions?

• •

Did you strike anyone?

• •

**Congratulations –
you're one step closer to becoming more Bercow.**

BONE-HEADED BERCOW

When the present-day speaker was not even twenty in 1981, and a politics student at the University of Essex, he shockingly stood for election to the national executive of the Monday Club. For those that don't know, this was and is a pressure group aligned to, but now not endorsed by, the Conservative Party that actively described itself as a 'guardian of the Tory conscience'. Founded in 1961 to try and move the party back to the right from its perceived shift to the left, it had since become obsessed with race politics. Bercow stood on a particularly offensive ticket, and produced a manifesto declaring, 'The strengthening of our national identity demands a programme of assisted repatriation.' He did not win the nomination but was an active member of the group until he left the following year.

Reportedly he has denounced his association with the Monday Club as 'utter madness' and described his views from that time as 'bone-headed'. And as a current champion of diversity in race, gender and sexuality, he seems to have performed a total U-turn. In fact, in 2009 he was the only Conservative to support Harriet Harman's legislation on equality and joined Diane Abbott to support all-black shortlists for seats in parliament.

'I feel very strongly that our opposition to racism and to sexism, and our support for *equality* before the law and an independent judiciary are hugely important considerations in the House of Commons.'

John Bercow,
February 2017

'Zen.
Restraint.
Patience.'

John Bercow,
January 2019

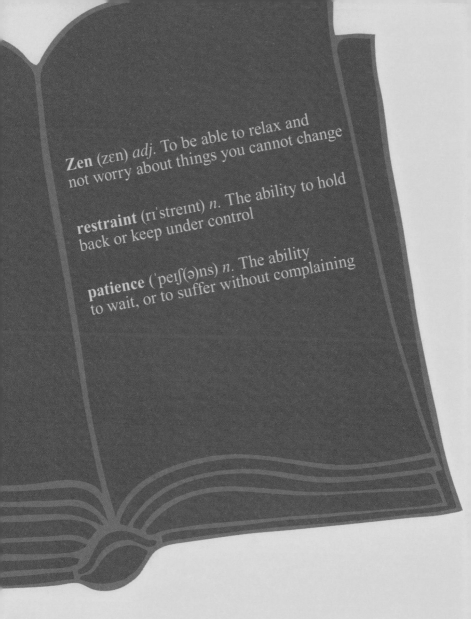

Zen (zɛn) *adj.* To be able to relax and not worry about things you cannot change

restraint (rɪˈstreɪnt) *n.* The ability to hold back or keep under control

patience (ˈpeɪʃ(ə)ns) *n.* The ability to wait, or to suffer without complaining

Mr Speaker's words are clearly wasted on his colleagues in the House of Commons, but why not try to apply his sage advice to the executive proceedings in your house?

SWINGER JOHN

As a former right-winger who has seemingly changed
his views towards a more left-wing set of values,
John Bercow has the ability to swing through
180 degrees and still remain upright.

On the next page use the 'Swingometer' to explore
any changes of opinion you've had over the years.

For example, maybe you once loved the music of Ed Sheeran,
but now you think it is anodyne elevator music.

$$(+) \cdot (X) \cdot (\div) = 💩$$

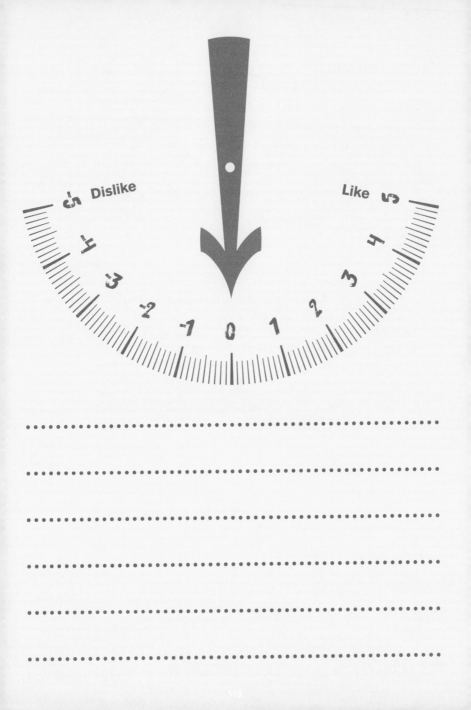

As Speaker of the House, John Bercow has to engage all his senses to fulfil his parliamentary function successfully.

SIGHT

to gauge Member's emotional state.

HEARING

to listen for insubordination.

SMELL

to detect which Members may be inebriated after lunch.

TASTE

to benchmark and reflect the public mood.

TOUCH

to use heavily or gently.

And of course his 'noes' and 'ayes' are vital sensory responses.

Appreciate your senses and see how they help in the running of your house.

SIGHT

....

HEARING

....

SMELL

....

TASTE

....

TOUCH

....

Scrutinizing our senses helps us to engage with them better.

'Mr Gove! You really are a very over-excitable individual. You need to write out 1,000 times, "I will behave myself at Prime Minister's Questions".'

John Bercow,
February 2014

OLD-SCHOOL STYLE

Mr Speaker made this comment to the then Education Secretary, mimicking the style of a school teacher. But these old-school disciplinary techniques may have some use on our path to enlightenment.

Why not take an area of your life that you would like to examine and improve upon, and distil this into a single memorable phrase.

....

....

Then write that phrase out 1,000 times, being mindful of your feelings as you do so.

The Charge of the Light Brigade
by Alfred, Lord Tennyson

I

Half a league, half a league,
Half a league onward,
All in the valley of Death
  Rode the six hundred.
'Forward, the Light Brigade!
Charge for the guns!' he said.
Into the valley of Death
  Rode the six hundred.

II

'Forward, the Light Brigade!'
Was there a man dismayed?
Not though the soldier knew
  Someone had blundered.
  Theirs not to make reply,
  Theirs not to reason why,
  Theirs but to do and die.
  Into the valley of Death
  Rode the six hundred.

III

Cannon to right of them,
Cannon to left of them,
Cannon in front of them
  Volleyed and thundered;
Stormed at with shot and shell,
Boldly they rode and well,
Into the jaws of Death,
Into the mouth of hell
  Rode the six hundred.

IV

Flashed all their sabres bare,
Flashed as they turned in air
Sabring the gunners there,
Charging an army, while
  All the world wondered.
Plunged in the battery-smoke
Right through the line they broke;
Cossack and Russian
Reeled from the sabre stroke
  Shattered and sundered.
Then they rode back, but not
  Not the six hundred.

V

Cannon to right of them,
Cannon to left of them,
Cannon behind them
  Volleyed and thundered;
Stormed at with shot and shell,
While horse and hero fell.
They that had fought so well
Came through the jaws of Death,
Back from the mouth of hell,
All that was left of them,
  Left of six hundred.

VI

When can their glory fade?
O the wild charge they made!
  All the world wondered.
Honour the charge they made!
Honour the Light Brigade,
  Noble six hundred!

BERCOW'S LOVE MATCH

Famed for his love of football, and in particular Arsenal FC, Mr Speaker
has also had a lifelong love affair with tennis. As a boy he was a
prodigious talent, and then as a young man he qualified as a coach,
but as his political career took off he put down the racket until his
election as an MP in 1997 when he joined the Commons tennis team.
Partnered with a dynamic left-hander, David Cameron MP, the two were
a formidable pair. But, as with many great collaborations, over time
their union turned to what many have called a feud.

As a backbencher in 2005 Bercow had described the Cameron-directed
Conservative manifesto as 'embarassingly thin', and then as Speaker
during the six years of Cameron's premiership there were many
accusations from the Tory party faithful that he was very quick to
cut the PM's speeches short. As with many feuds, things seemed
to fizzle out, but John Bercow's passion for tennis remains,
with him regularly sprinkling references to his favourite
player Roger Federer into Commons debate.

'I always say the best thing about Switzerland is not its watches, its financial services or its chocolate; the best thing about Switzerland is Roger Federer.'

John Bercow,
March 2019

'None of you
is a traitor.'

John Bercow,
March 2019

TRAITOR MANTRA

Have you ever felt betrayed?

Have you ever been called a traitor?

Have you ever called someone a traitor?

In these politically polemical times our feelings and emotions can run away with themselves, and we must sometimes step back from words said and deeds done, and seek solace.

Find a peaceful space, relax into a cross-legged meditation pose, and repeat this mantra...

NONE OF US IS A TRAITOR

Next time Parliament is in session, challenge a friend to

BERCOW BINGO!

ORR-DERR!	MR PETER BONE	MEDICAMENT
THE NOES HAVE IT	YOGA	LOCK
LET IT GO	CHATTEL	ZEN
RESTRAINT	BREXIT	ROGER FEDERER

Mark off the words as Mr Speaker goes about
his business, and when you have them all shout

'FULL HOUSE (OF COMMONS)'

UNLOCK	CALM	ARSENAL
GET A GRIP	THANGAM DEBBONAIRE	ORR-DERR!
MEDICAMENT	PATIENCE	THE AYES HAVE IT
WIMBLEDON	MANTRA	OATH OF ALLEGIANCE

THE WIMBLEDON MANDALA

As a self-confessed tennis addict and author of a book on the top 20 male players of all time, John Bercow is regularly spotted in the Royal Box at the annual Wimbledon Championships.

When you need a bit more calm and order in your life, be more Bercow and focus your attentions on this mandala inspired by the Wimbledon Championships.